Pets and their Celebrities

Animal Fair

Animal Fair Media, Inc. titles may be purchased for business or promotional use or for special sales. For information, please write to: Special Markets Department
545 Eighth Avenue, New York, NY 10018

Library of Congress Cataloging-in-Publication number: 2001090017

ISBN 0964731622

UPC 719340-55555-1

FIRST EDITION

Photographs by Christopher Ameruoso

Book and cover design by Michelle Bada

Printed in Hong Kong by Colorprint Offset

LAST CHANCE FOR ANIMALS
www.LCAnimal.org

a portion of the author's proceeds for the sale of this book will be contributed to Last Chance for Animals

How do you begin to talk about someone for whom you have so much respect and admiration? I will begin with the word 'dedication'. How many times in one's life can he say that he has really been dedicated to something? I mean, giving it his all, one hundred percent of his heart and soul; it's questionable. Is there anything in your life for which you would do absolutely anything? How about commiting your life to saving that of an animal's? Maybe a creature you have never seen before, something that doesn't even belong to you. Something that someone else would pass up running in the street through a busy intersection. What about standing before a car driving toward you at 60 m.p..h. or even being sent away to prison for attempting to save one of these creatures? Would you take a bullet for the life of an animal? Most would say that this is absolutely crazy. I think that it is dedication to the maximum.

I have learned so much in the past year and a half about being dedicated to something that I truly believe in. I have watched someone work harder in a week than most people do in two months, run a business without an income. I think most of us would lose dedication pretty quickly. Not this person. His obstacles only seem to drive him more, push him harder to save more lives. This person has almost seemed to assume an animal instinct for survival. I guess this is why when you witness his encounters with animals, you can see that they bond very quickly. Whether it be the most viscious of dogs, or a frightened cat, this man can actually pet a fly. When I began this project, many people told me, 'It's really hard to get a book published, not to mention getting celebrities to let you photograph them when you're not a well-known photographer.' I took what I learned from this person about dedication and put it to use. The result is the culmination of my efforts in this amazing collection of photographs.

I would like to take this opportunity to dedicate this book to Chris DeRose, a man of strength and dignity. I have learned so much from his commitment to his convictions. I am now certain that I can accomplish anything with my newfound definition of the word 'dedication'.

Chris DeRose, this book is for you.

I also appreciate this opportunity to honor two of the most amazing people I know. These two have proven that there is hope for the American family. 'Through sickness and in health, through good times and bad, for richer and poorer,' they have been put to the test and have survived. They are my two greatest role models. Respect is the starting point and the finish for everything we do in life. I moved from New York to Los Angeles ten years ago, and one of the most difficult things I had to do was to leave my family behind. I received nothing but support and respect from these two people.

I would, therefore, also like to dedicate this book to both my mother and my father for raising me with trust, love and respect. I love you both dearly ...

Introduction

I originally came up with the concept for this book in December 1998. Yes, I know what you are saying, "that's a long time." I have had people tell me that they have produced and filmed motion pictures in the time I have taken to produce this book. My response, 'well, in a movie you have only to deal with two or three celebrities. My book has about eighty.' Living in Los Angeles, I see quite a few celebrities wandering around with their pets. I can also feel the love and see a different side of each person. So, what I wanted to do was to photograph everyone in black and white at home in a very comfortable environment. I wanted to capture the love and true bond between the person and the animal.

My first photo shoot was with Janeane Garofalo. I guess that is why I felt so compelled to have her photos first in this book. The pictures turned out to be amazing, just the way I had envisioned them. So, for the next two years I was the king of mingle, quick-draw photographer. I was very fortunate to receive a positive response from just about everyone I approached. You will even find celebrities in this book that do not own a pet, but were kind enough to pose with one that was rescued.

So, now I have these wonderful photos of people and their animals, and I started to think to myself, 'Self, is this how it's supposed to happen? You have grown all of your life playing music in a band. You move to Los Angeles ten years ago with a dream of music and all of a sudden you have fallen into a career that you had never even thought about until now.' Then, I really began to wonder when a photographer friend of mine asked, "When did you become a professional photographer?" My response, 'What is professional, anyway?' I thought that maybe being a "professional" meant you had to be in the business for at least ten years and have been paid for your work, and possibly know the lingo. Well, I didn't let this deter me, so I went on.

What was my next step? I was just about halfway through the shooting when I met Joanne Wiles. Joanne is one of those people who when she says she will do something for you, she really means it. Considering Joanne is with the William Morris Agency, this was pretty much what I needed to get a publishing deal for the book. Well, it wasn't really that simple. I kind of felt like I was thrown back in the old days with the band trying to get a record deal. You know, sending out demos and getting passed on. It was beginning to become all too familiar again when receiving pass letters from publishing companies. That is, until a bite came along from a very renowned publisher.

Great, so now the process starts, meeting everyone and selling my concept to them. Needless to say, I did. Imagine sitting in a room with ten heads of a very large publishing company. Well, I strutted my stuff. And now I had a publishing deal. Well, that didn't last too long, on account of "artistic differences". I had a decision to make ... leave the company and start over, or, stay, bite the bullet and let someone else take the heart out of what I had created over the past two years. Ah, no, for the good of the book, I left. Would you believe, the very day I left, I found an amazing publishing company to put out this book, Animal Fair Media. This is a group of people headed by Wendy Diamond who has the same sized heart as mine for animals and the nature of this book. I was the luckiest guy in the world. So, the work went on and we talked and pulled this project together.

Everyone I have encountered along the way has truly been amazing in lending a helping hand. I am very fortunate to have had these people involved. I am a firm believer now that if you do put your mind to something and really stick with it, the reward is there to be received. As a Pisces, I have a tendency to put my hands in everything. Well, I finally stuck my hand in the right box and had the opportunity to work with all these talented and beautiful people. I hope you will enjoy what you see in this book and feel the warmth and love that human beings have for their pets, and the animals for their owners. I truly believe that you begin to resemble your animal after a while. I think you will see this in many of these photos. I would also like to add to all of those hopefuls out there (and I know there are many of you, because I am many of you), please follow your dreams and always go with your gut instinct. It will always end up being right, and you will be rewarded in the end. I am incredibly grateful for everything that has happened to me over the past two years.

Christopher Ameruoso

Foreword

Who can explain the joy that a dog or a cat that loves you has given you? They can make or change your day; you can be blue and suddenly you're happy because of the spirit they inject in you.

People forget that pets are a strong dynamic of life, and to some people, they're no different to them than their own children. I have known more people in my life that have gotten joy and pleasure and a life worth living out of a relationship with a particular animal, whether it be a dog, a cat, a horse, or a mouse.

They are part of our lives and we have to appreciate them as part of our lives. Every animal has their own personality and reason why they appeal to you just like every person does. There is little difference in that approach. You have affection and affinity for an animal as you would a friend.

I am grateful to Chris DeRose for founding Last Chance for Animals and to Christopher Ameruoso for his efforts in raising awareness for this worthwhile cause. But, mostly, I am grateful to all those little creatures that have been a source of laughter, joy, and inspiration throughout my life.

← Dew

Rescued at aprox 6 weeks

Dew

Janeane Garofalo

Walter, Wallingford -
He's as clever as a puppy can be
Walter, Wallingford
He's got a masters and a PHD

He's a rolly polly fatty
He's a cool dog Daddy
Looking sharp in coat & tail
He's never garrulous or trite
He's got his own web site
Picasso did his collar
He's a mensa scholar

Walter, Wallingford
He's got a scholarship to MIT
Majoring in Algebra
with a minor in poop and pee

Walter

William H. Macy, Felicity Huffman

Bisou

Rosanna Arquette

Big Sweet Dumb Brilliant Love.

Annie and Buddy

Lisa Rinna

Nala and Zac

Rachel Hunter

DEAN GOT BOSCO FOR FREE FROM THE BACKEND OF A PICKUP!

JAY HAD BEEN ABUSED, BUT WAS THEN RESCUED BY HIS REAL SUPERHERO, DADDY DEAN CAIN. HE IS THE FIRST DOG DEAN HAS EVER HAD.

IN MEMORIAM

Jay
_____
Dean Cain

"Cifi is the most notable dog that I have ever known. He will protect me with his life, as he has been trained to do. Yet, he is my favorite companion."

"He tolerates other people so politely and even makes them think that he likes them. But, he really doesn't. He only has eyes for me"

Cifi

Bo Derek

KITTY DOES NOT WATCH T.V.
SHE'S A REAL SOUL. SHE STILL
READS BOOKS.

Kitty

Natasha Henstridge

RENO WAS RESCUED by JAMES WHILE ON THE SET OF "MISERY".

Reno

James Caan

Sebastian found a lizard and was playing soccer with it on the floor in the kitchen. I rescued the lizard just in time.

Sebastian sleeps with me - but he SNORES!

Sebastian

Angelica Bridges

some other pet

Mr. Freeze

Slash

Gart

Tippi Hedren

Keiko

Rob Lowe

Keiko's owners,
Kimberly Von Hagen
and Alex Baik

"FRACK"

EVERYONE ALWAYS ASKS ME "WHERE'S FRICK"?
HERE'S THE STORY.....

ONCE A PON A TIME THERE WAS A FRICK & FRACK!
ONE DAY FRACK DECIDED TO PICK A FIGHT
WITH FRICK. FRACK EARNED HIS THRONE. FRICK
THEN TOLD MOMMY, BY TURNING BLACK, (AND HE
IS A GREEN IGUANA) THAT HE MIGHT PREFER
A BETTER HOME. FRACK MAY HAVE WON HIS THRONE,
BUT FRICK IS NOW HAPPY BEING ALONE! AND NOW
FRACK JUST BEATS UP ON MOMMY — AND THAT'S THE STORY

Frack

DeDee Pfeiffer

Bug and Fester

Rose McGowan

Caprichoso

Tatjana Patitz

When she trys to get something from me,
she talks to me like CHEWBACCA

Kahlua
Christine Taylor

Elle
Ben Stiller

Jan Andrieu, Elle's owner

Foo

Dustin Nguyen, Pamela Anderson, and Natalie

Star

Natalie Raitano

he growls when you scratch his ears

Star

Pamela Anderson

187 and Assasin

Ice-T

Oliver is a fluffy adorable mutt who is
somewhat food obsessed and enjoys talk radio

Oliver

Elizabeth Barondes

Fargo

WAS PETUNIA RESCUED?

YES- FROM THE AMANDA FOUNDATION

Petunia

Illeana Douglas

my pets get groomed with love ery day   PAULIE

Archie and Butter

Paulie Shore

Buttwing and Casper

Diane Warren

(FEMALE)
Cuca Hannibal (male)

Cuca and Hannibal

David Alan Grier

Lulu, Pablo, Stella

WHY THOSE NAMES?

YOU JUST WAIT A BIT, CALL 'EM "DOG"
+ EVENTUALLY A NAME WILL COME TO YOU. *Kristen*

Pablo

Kristen Johnston

Orsin

Vincent Schiavelli

I dreamed of a beautiful creature.
She came to me in
pictures and paintings,
wishes and dreams.
Then, one day in Japan,
On the streets of Shinjuku,
she appeared.
Her eyes called out to me
full of love.
It was destined to be.
I fell in love with Poppy.

Lisa Marie

Poppy

Lisa Marie

Zero

Jack Skellington and Sally

sketches by Tim Burton

IF LORETTA WERE A STAR, WHO WOULD SHE B

Loretta: Dolly Parton
(WHITE)

HOW ABOUT DOLORES?

Dolores: KEELY Smith
(BLACK)

DO YOUR DOGS SLEEP IN BED WITH YOU?

we'll never tell...

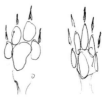

Loretta and Delores

Deborah Mazar

Shadow

Garcelle Beauvais

Yogi and Amy

N a l a

Amy Smart

Bizkit
Fred Durst

Max Luca

Shannen Doherty

Ella

Courteney Cox Arquette and David Arquette

Cleopold

Gina Gershon

"A victim of ignorance and displacement, sadly, innocent, Wiley languished on death row in the pound until almost her final day. Then she met the pretty lady with blue eyes, and instantly they fell in love. In return, she introduced her to the big nice guy who also has blue eyes, but not as pretty. They fell in love, too."

"Lucy's infancy was in East L.A. where she met the nice big guy on a film set. She showed her affection by peeing on him and he took her home to meet the pretty lady with blue eyes. They instantly fell in love, although, the big yellow dog was wary, at first ..."

Lucy and Wiley

Brendan and Afton Fraser

WHAT KIND OF CAR WOULD MISS ASHAP DRIVE? a vintage Jaguar

Miss Ochay

Sheryl Lee

"MY SWEET STITCH"

BETTER TO HAVE
A RAT IN YOUR
LIFE THAT LOVES YOU
THAN A RAT IN
YOUR LIFE THAT DOESN'T....

Michael Des Barres....

Stitch

Michael Des Barres

Ophelia

Mariska Hargitay

Snoopy

Ashley Hamilton and *Sara Foster*

He Sings - just like his mommy!

Ginger, Tyler, and Snappy

Wild Orchid

Stephanie Ridel, Renee Sandstrom, and Stacy Ferguson

 dumb blonde with a heart of gold

Angel kitty from hell

Boots

Alison Eastwood

Bogie

Paul Stanley

Curly Sue

Paula Abdul

CHARLES MONTANA is filed as my
first officer in the LEAR 25 N// ly
to Livingston MONTANA where I live
HE is the only dog to be so certified

Charles Montana

Harv Presnell

GERONIMO IS A GOOD LISTENER

THEIR FAVORITE TOY IS ME!

Geronimo

Nicollette Sheridan

Loverboy

Nicollette Sheridan

ALIK=HUMAN   LILA=OUT OF CONTROL

← JOE PESCHI

← DENIRO

WHAT IS ALIK and LILA'S FAVORITE FOOD? PIZZA CRUST

Alik and Lila

Brian Green

Mama's girl

Lady Like Person with lots of attitude

Nana

Kate Hudson

Cooper was rescued...
and found me actually...
in Hollywood...
I mean the middle of Hollywood!

human

gorgeous

eyes·eyes·eyes!

Cooper's friend, Zander

Cooper

Joely Fisher

Cosette, Edie, Jack, Rooney and Vincent

Connie Stevens

Ted and Clint

Sharing our lives with Five furry friends (And counting) has enriched our hearts & souls daily with their extreme personalities from the very particular OTIS, 13 who acts as the family's old time Don having complete control of us. Simon is the unconditional lover. (He's known to be a favorite) ??? Prince JASPER is a wildman and the adventurer and quite "a little Devil." Clint AKA "THE SHADOW" is always right under your nose just waiting to help out. Finally, my man MY first, TEDDY LEATHER. THE TRUE LEADER ONE GREAT BIG HEART

THE PRIDE AND JOY OF OUR Home

OUR CHILDREN   XO,

Otis

Jason Wiles

Stella

Julianne Moore

Stella's owner, Christopher Ameruoso

Kaanaloa: IT'S HAWAIIAN FOR : GOD OF THE OCEANS

Jackson, Kaanaloa and Sybil

Christina Applegate

Bonus

Bunker

Kaya

Mona

Bernie Taupin

Tess

Bosco's Salmon Supper

1 cup salmon skin & trimmings
1 cup brown rice (cooked according to directions)
1 cup mixed frozen veggies or leftover veggies from dinner
1/3 cup broth or water seasoned with bouillon
2 tablespoons olive oil
dash salt

Pre heat broiler to 300 degrees F. In pan or cookie sheet lined with foil, coat
with 1 tablespoon oil. Place salmon skin in pan, lightly salt, then place pan
under broiler and bake for 15 minutes or until crispy. While salmon is cooking,
place veggies in a saucepan with remaining oil and broth. Saute veggies until
tender, 5 to 10 minutes. Add rice and stir. * I always keep cooked brown rice
on hand. Remove salmon from oven and let cool for 5 minutes. Then cut or
tear into 1 inch pieces and mix with veggies and rice concoction. When cooled
to touch, it is ready to serve. Feeds 2 medium dogs.

Note: The salmon skin is usually trimmed from 1 pound of salmon filets bought
at the market. When we have salmon, so do the dogs.

Bosco

Faith Ford

Lulu

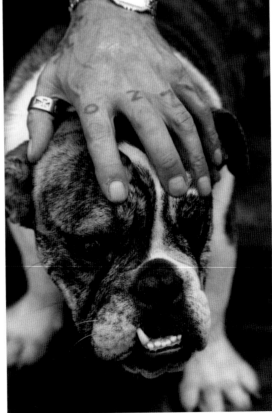

Frenchy

Chewy

Ozzy Osbourne

Penny ♡

My Baby, my most stable friend,
always there, always happy, nothing but
— pure luv —
We have been through it all together...
break-ups, wisdom teeth, braces, graduation,
death, many colds and flus, many vacations,
bad friends, bad boyfriends, many
ruined shoes, ruined carpets... EVERYTHING!
God willing, much more to come.
Penny, you R my heart, your little body
walks around with mommy's heart inside
you. the fuckin best!
my
Bitch! 4-life
♡ MAMA

Penny

Kidada Jones

Roger Toes

Monkey

Kari Wuhrer

Jack, Joey, Blue, and Ginger

Elvis and Ms. Kitty

Angie Everhart

William, Cleo, Bobbi Goldin, and Caliban

Cleo

William Atherton

he was filthy and soulful when i found him on the STREETS of HOLLYWOOD

Muddy

Anthony Kiedis

Memish, Georgia, Teddy, Samba, and Baby

Jillian Barberi

Kitty

Sally Kellerman

Owner, George Michael

Hugg

Geri Haliwell

Jennifer Lothrop

Robbie Williams

Sugar Ray

Harold and Susan Becker

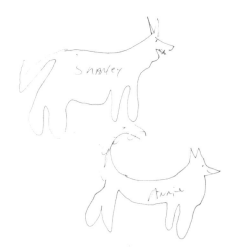

Annie and Sharkey

Scott Baio

WOOF
XXX

Woof

Phil and Anita Collen

SAM PUT HIS PAWS AROUND HIS WATER BOWL,

STUCK HIS FACE IN AND BLEW BUBBLES

THROUGH HIS NOSE

THANK YOU FOR RESCUING ME

Buster and Sam

Maureen O'Boyle

MY GOOD FRIEND

Isabel

Jeffrey Tambor

Found several days after the last big Los Angeles earthquake

Sally Struthers

Happy Hattie

Sally Struthers

Atlanta, John, Zoe, and Jack

Jack

John Taylor

Stella

Cheri Oteri

Bear

Joel West

Acknowledgements

First and foremost, I would like to acknowledge my family: Mother, Father, Vito, Frank, Martin, Joanne, Rocky Sr., Lisa, Liz, Rocky Jr., Anthony, Lauren, Christian, Amanda, and Kristin. How can I begin to thank you all for the support and love you have given me throughout the years? I love you.

Tracey Ross, you have helped me tremendously with this book and I want to thank you for all of the great people you have introduced me to since I have known you. You made things alot easier and I love you like my own sister. You are one of the most generous people I know.

Janey Lopaty, you were there with me from the beginning and stuck with me. Thank you for your great sense of style and help with this book.

Bobbi Baird, I have known you since my journey to Los Angeles started, and I will know you for the rest of my life. Thank you for all the time you have donated and for your great makeup work. Most of all, thank you for being a great friend.

Karen Zambos, thank you so much for the help you have given me with this project. Your friendship means alot to me. I am glad you are in my life.

Helena Peterson, you always have a way of making me smile, and that's one of the most important factors of a friendship. I am really thrilled to have you as a part of my life.

Jonathan West, for all your great outtake photos and for the great photos of my little girl and myself, thank you so much. "I kissed Bo Derek."

Anthony Albano, we have been here in Los Angeles for ten years and it has been pretty rough at times, but we survived. I am glad you are my friend and I know this will all be worth the pain we have been through. Thank you for bringing New York pizza to L.A. "Albanos rules." Thanks for the help with the shoots and for the support you have given me.

Louis Albano, thank you for the help you have given me with the shoots, and for all of your support.

To the Zazzaro family, I just want you to know how much I appreciate all of the support you have given me throughout the years. I know I have taken some turns in my career, but that's me. It was truly a great day when your family moved across the street from mine. Thank you ...

Dawn, for all the years you have been there, I wanted to let you know how much I appreciate your friendship. Thank you.

Ru Diaz, thank you for all of your support and for being there when I needed someone to talk to.

Natalie Raitano, I want to thank you for the help you have given me with this book. I am so proud of your career and especially your kindness. I truly appreciate what you have done.

Summer Rush, for your support and for taking my teasing. Thanks.

I want to give a very special thank you to Joanne Wiles for offering to help with this project and in getting this book published. From the day I met you, and you said that you would help, you really pulled through and kept your word. I don't know how I would have done this without you. Thank you ...

Jan and everyone at Control Multi Media, what can I say about the amazing web site you have created for me? It truly brings out the spirit of this book. Thank you.

Johnny Mac thank you for all the great years of friendship and support you are truly my best friend.

Wendy Diamond, you are a true savior. Thank you believing in this book and for your true talent for bringing Animal Fair to the public. We need a little more tenderness in our lives like you show us in your magazine. This world would be a much better place. Thank you.

Luisa Nunez, for all your great creativity and talent and for putting up with all of my phone calls, thank you.

Cindy Newman, I want to tell you that I appreciate your friendship and for being there when I need you.

To everyone at Last Chance for Animals, you people are the true heroes, for all of the endless hours you put into saving the lives of all the abused animals in this world that can't help themselves. I applaud all of you ...

Claudia Jaffee, thank you for all the wonderful advice you give me. I admire your sense of business. Thank you for your support.

Stacey Griffith, to the coolest lady I know, thank you for all of your support. You are a very special person in my life.

Sven Petersen, thank you so much for all your help with the prints for this book. You have a great eye for a great photo.

Michael Des Barres, thanks for the support you have given me and for your inspirational talks. You truly are one of the most talented people I know.

Rosanna Arquette, I am truly honored to have been able to photograph one of the most beautiful people I know.

Kari Wuhrer, you know how I feel about you. Now I get to put it in writing permanently. I love you. Thank you for everything.

To all of the publicists and agents who helped in allowing your truly talented clients to be photographed. Thank you.

Mr. John Travolta, I want to thank you for your heartfilled foreward. It is truly an honor.

Leanne Magraw, I found my soulmate in you. I love you. God really has blessed me by putting you in my life.

Michelle Parker, thank you for taking care of my pride and joy (Stella) and for all of your support.

To all of the people who let me photograph your pets that you have rescued. God bless you for your compassion in saving these beautiful creatures. To all of the celebrities, there is no book without your wonderful faces. Thank you all from the bottom of my heart.

Claudia Cross, thank you for putting up with all my phone calls and for making this book come to life.

Rhea Rachevsky and everyone at Art Mix, thank you all for your help and support. It has been a long hard road, but finally it is complete.

Jillian Barberie, how can I thank you enough for all your support? I am glad we became friends. Thank you.

Efrain Padilla and everyone at CM Color Labs, this book truly would not have been done without your support and great work. The endless photos and time you have put out into this project are truly amazing. You have brought life to what I saw through the lens of my camera. I will never be able to thank you enough.

Nicollette Sheridan, I want to tell you that I truly appreciate all that you have done for me. Thank you for letting me share your beautiful images with the world.

Michelle Bada, what can I say about all of the hard work you have put into the layout of this book? You truly put your heart and soul into everything you have done. You should be very proud of this book because I know that I am. Thank you.

Stella

About 12 1/4 inches tall, skin like a nerf sponge, wiry white stringy hair ... this is Stella. Straight out of a Dr. Seuss novel, "What is Stella?". Is it a dog, is it a cat? A rat? Or, just some kind of extraterrestrial? Where does she come from? Was she really bred for the Chinese monks as a bed warmer, or was she just a science project gone terribly wrong? Whatever or wherever she hales from, words cannot explain the personality of this 7 1/2 pound creature. Aware of all of the stares and attention she attracts, she expects you to stop in the street and pet her bare body in return for a smile that she will put on your face. Oh, and if you hadn't noticed her, she will make her presence known by standing on hind leg much like the meir cat.

I wish I had a dime for every time I have answered, "it's not a haircut. It's natural." She is a Chinese Crested. A Chinese what? Is it my New York accent, or is it those two words that just don't sound quite right together? Chinese Crested.

Whatever, wherever, or whoever she is, Stella is my best friend, my child. It may be difficult to realize how much joy one can get out of something that can nearly fit in one hand. Another of God's superb creations, Stella Blue.

photo credit Jonathan West